Mormonism's Colorful Cowboy

J. Golden Kimball Stories

by

James Kimball

with illustrations by

Pat Bagley

Salt Lake City 1999

Cover Art and Design by Pat Bagley

**Edited by: Linda Bult, Marti Esplin
and Jennifer Sokolowsky**

ISBN: 1-566845491

10 9 8 7 6 5 4 3

Mormonism's Colorful Cowboy

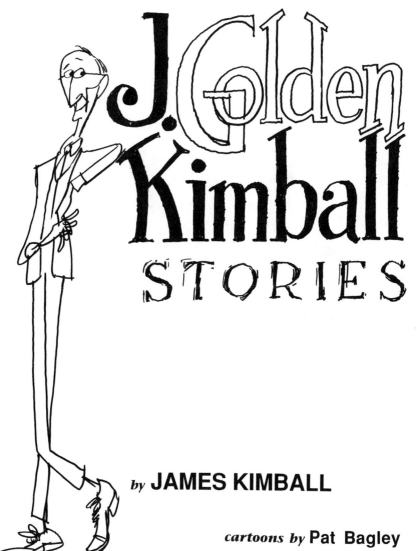

J. Golden Kimball STORIES

by **JAMES KIMBALL**

cartoons by **Pat Bagley**

ACKNOWLEDGMENTS

I want to thank all the kind men and women who take the time to tell me their favorite J. Golden Kimball stories. Even now, sixty years after his death, people still come up with stories about Uncle Golden, told and preserved in their families, that are new and delightfully surprising to me. I am grateful, of course, to my Uncle Golden. Without his life and wit there never would have been a book of amusing stories. I need to thank Fred Esplin, Elizabeth Searles and all the other wise, witty and wonderful people at KUED who helped produce the J. Golden Kimball videos.

To Joan, Ted, John and Amy — I hope this book in some way explains my absence from your lives of late.

— James Kimball

INTRODUCTION

J. Golden Kimball looked unique. He was 6-foot-4, skinny as a beanpole, and spoke in a high-pitched voice.

He was unique.

In 170 years, the Mormon Church hasn't produced another leader quite like him. He swore like a cowboy (which he was), occasionally drank coffee, had a lightning-quick wit, and loved the Gospel with all his heart.

In these pages is the most complete (and humorous) volume of J. Golden stories you'll ever run across.

James Kimball, best known for playing his famous relative on two award-winning PBS specials, "Remembering Uncle Golden" and "On the Road With Uncle Golden," retells story after story gleaned from family and Mormon lore. These are stories that have been passed down around campfires, dinner tables and in sacrament meetings for almost a century.

AUTHOR'S NOTE

J. Golden Kimball was a General Authority for over 50 years beginning in the 1890s. General Authorities are the ruling body of the Mormon Church. In a church noted for its reverential leaders, J. Golden stuck out like an irreverent sore thumb.

He was a cowboy Christian who preached the Gospel with wit, compassion, and a sometimes colorful vocabulary. He was like a fresh breeze on a dry prairie. Back then, the members of the Church loved him. They still do.

Golden was my great-grand uncle — my grandfather Abraham Alonzo Kimball's half brother. (Since I'm on the subject of family relations, I might as well mention here that another famous Kimball, Spencer W., was Golden's nephew).

I have pulled together these stories from hundreds of conversations with family members, cowboys, farmers, housewives, college professors, bricklayers, nurses, vegetarians, veterinarians and a myriad of other kind people.

This book did not require a great deal of effort. I simply took all the stories from my two KUED videos, "Remembering Uncle Golden" and "On The Road With Uncle Golden," edited them, added a few stories I had been told since the last taping and handed them over to Pat Bagley and Margaret Reiser. The book was their idea. I should like to thank them for their creativity and hard work in getting this ready for publication.

They are two people of equally pleasant dispositions who care as I do to keep alive the memory of a man who was not afraid to be himself. He is worth remembering because his plain-spoken truths made people laugh — primarily at themselves.

— James Kimball

Those that I like and admire I can find no common denominator. But those that I love, I can. They all make me laugh.

- W. H. Audin

EARLY GOLDEN

J. Golden Kimball was born in 1853 in the Utah territory to Christine Kimball. His father was Brigham Young's right-hand man, Heber C. Kimball. When Golden was 15, Heber died and the family — his mother, brother and sister — moved to a small ranch near Bear Lake in northern Utah. It was a tough, hardscrabble existence where the young Golden learned ranching, farming, cowboying and how to motivate mules by hurling memorable words at them at high velocity.

TALK TO THE ANIMALS

"People say I shouldn't swear. I don't mean to, brothers and sisters. It just comes out. They're left over from my cowboy days. That experience made me as tough as a pine knot. You can't drive mules if you can't swear. It's the only language they understand. I do swear a little, but they're just small leftovers from a far larger vocabulary!"

HEBER C. KIMBALL

I KEEP PICTURES OF THE BOYS IN MY OTHER WALLET.

I REMEMBER PAPA

"My father was a wonderful man, a great Church leader. He had 43 wives, 46 sons and 22 daughters. He never mentioned any of these figures to Mother, and neither did I."

HOPE THEY SEND
ME ON A MISSION (NOT!)

When Golden turned 30, his mother asked him to consider going on a mission. Golden was lukewarm to the notion. But he promised he would go see President John Taylor about it the next time he was in Salt Lake. But, he said, "If he doesn't think I would make a good missionary, then I won't go!" She agreed.

Golden had a plan. Over the next two weeks he didn't bathe or shave. When he got ready to go, he put on cowboy boots that were covered in manure, a filthy pair of chaps, a stained shirt, two six-guns on his hips and a Bowie knife stuck in his belt.

When he arrived in Salt Lake, he tied up his horse in front of the Beehive House and walked into President Taylor's office. He said, "Is there someone named Taylor here?" Immediately the president jumped up, shook his hand and said, "Brother Kimball, I just read your mother's letter and I know, just like your father, you will make a great missionary for the Church!"

Golden fell back on his next line of defense. "I

would be happy to go, President, but I have no money." President Taylor looked out the window and said, "I was just looking at that

beautiful horse, saddle, bridle and blanket. Isn't that yours?" Golden said, yes, it was. Taylor told him to go to the livery stable and sell everything. "That will give you enough money for your mission."

Golden did as instructed. He gave Taylor all the money. The president counted it out. "We'll send you a few dollars every month. Now here's a little extra — go over to ZCMI and buy a suit and some shirts."

In a few hours Golden came back looking every inch the skinny ambassador of the restored Gospel he'd be to the Southern States.

MISSION

In April 1883, Golden was sent to the Southern States Mission, which consisted of most of the old Confederacy. It was a scant 18 years after the Civil War. Feelings still ran high against carpet-bagging Yankees, and Mormon missionaries were sometimes beaten, tarred and feathered, or even killed.

Besides hostile "natives," Golden had to struggle with his own sense of unworthiness as he went about the Lord's business.

IGNERNT

"I didn't know much about the Gospel. As a matter of fact, when I left on my mission I was a complete ignoramus. I thought epistles were wives of apostles."

MUST BE TRUE

"The Gospel must be true or greenhorn missionaries, like me, would have ruined it long time ago."

THE HIGH
COST OF DYING

Golden contracted yellow fever on his mission and almost died. B. H. Roberts, who was the acting mission president, came to see him. He said, "Brother Kimball, you look really ill. You ought to go home."

Golden looked simply awful, but he put the best face on the situation. "Hell, I've always looked this way. I appreciate your concern, but I'd prefer to stay."

Roberts said, "Well, Brother Kimball, it's an economic consideration: if we can send you home alive, it costs us $53.18. If you die on us, it's $112.42."

Golden responded, "I want to stay, Elder Roberts. If I die, I will pay the difference!"

GOLDEN, YOU DON'T LOOK SO GOOD...

D.O.A.

DOESN'T TAKE A FORTUNE TELLER

Golden seemed to be losing his bout with yellow fever. Twenty-two precious pounds had melted from his already skinny frame. He went to see a doctor.

"The doctor told me I was going to die if I didn't get well, which was an interesting observation."

He recovered, no thanks to the doctor.

HAREM SCARE 'EM

There were ministers of religion in the South who were telling everybody, "The Mormon missionaries are here for one reason — they're here to steal your wives and your daughters and take them back to live in polygamy!"

Golden found the notion absurd. "All you had to do was look at those women and know that thought never would have crossed our minds."

MY TWO SONS

The Rev. Charles A. Weatherbee was a popular Baptist minister who went throughout the Deep South spreading lies about the Mormons.

Golden encountered him as a young elder in Memphis, Tennessee. He and his companion were walking down the street, and coming from the other direction was Rev. Weatherbee. Golden nudged his companion, "Isn't that the man who preaches against us?" His companion said, "Yes, that's him."

As Weatherbee got nearer, he recognized the two ragtag young men in ill-fitting suits carrying valises as Mormon elders. Righteous wrath suddenly darkened the minister's features. "Good morning, you sons of the Devil!" he growled.

Golden doffed his hat politely and said, "Good morning, father!"

MISSION II

*After he was released from his mission, Golden
came home, married Jennie Knowlton and
began a family in Logan, Utah. He was called
to work in the YMMIA throughout the stake and
went into the farm implement business. For the
first time in his life, he had a little change in his
pocket. Golden looked forward to settling into a
life of relative prosperity.*

God had other plans for Golden.

NO HORSING AROUND

A letter from President Wilford Woodruff arrived. He asked Golden to come down to Salt Lake. "So I rode my horse down, but this time I tied him up three blocks away from the president's office."

Not that it did any good. The president asked Golden to accept the calling of president of the Southern States Mission. Golden accepted.

LET THE LORD SORT IT OUT

Unlike today, mission presidents back in the early days of the Church went without their families. Seeing Golden off at the train station was President Woodruff.

As they stood on the platform waiting for the call to board, President Woodruff put his arm around Golden, and asked, "Brother Kimball, I've never been to the Southern States. What's it like? Tell me about the people of the South. I understand the Civil War changed them. What are your thoughts?"

Golden hadn't seen the Southerners at their best. He had been chased, insulted and assaulted while on his first mission. Once they even put him in an iron cage and hung it from a tree so folks could get a good look at a real, live Mormon. Dixie had severely tested his Christian charity. "President," he said, "if I had my way, I'd drown them all and do baptismal work for the dead."

Golden later recalled that President Woodruff gave him the strangest look he'd ever received.

WHEREVER YOU GO, THERE YOU ARE

Back in his old missionary stomping grounds, Golden once more ran into the Reverend Weatherbee. This time the two were scheduled to engage in a debate. This took place in a crowded public meeting in Chattanooga.

The Reverend was the first to speak. He went on and on about how all the Mormons were going to go to Hell if they didn't change their ways. "They don't have the truth, they're going straight to Hell! This is a good man," he said, pointing to Golden, "but he's going straight to Hell!" He spoke for over an hour and didn't vary once from his "Straight to Hell" theme.

Finally it was Golden's turn. He could tell the audience was restless, so he said, "I only have one thing to say. I'd rather be a Mormon going to Hell than not be a Mormon and not know where the hell I'm going!" Then he sat down.

The crowd jumped to its feet and cheered. It was the best sermon they'd heard in a long time and did a lot to improve people's opinions about the Mormons.

DIRTY LINEN
IN PUBLIC

The most difficult thing Golden faced on his second mission was harassment by the Ku Klux Klan. Along with Jews, Catholics and African Americans, Mormons were targets for tar and feathering, whippings, and murder. In the years following the Civil War, the Klan was a powerful and intimidating force in the Old South.

"Waste of a good sheet," was Golden's opinion.

DUMB KLUX

In the fall of 1891, Golden received a telegram saying the Klan was going to tar and feather all the elders in that county if they did not leave immediately. Golden instructed all the elders to meet outside Rome, Georgia.

He met the elders as planned and they went into the hills to hold their meeting. It was in a clearing next to a large stream in the Georgia pines. The night was clear and the moon was out. They built a large fire, had a word of prayer and began a testimony meeting.

Golden was the last to speak. He had only said a few words when they heard horses coming up on the far side of the stream. By the light of the moon they could see the Klan's white sheets. They had a wagon with a big cauldron on it. Golden kept talking to the elders as the Klan war-whooped it up and built a big fire. They unloaded the wagon and put the cauldron on the fire.

Soon the pungent aroma of tar filled the trees. Golden saw fear on the missionary's faces but said, "Elders, don't you worry about a thing. I was raised around scum like that, I know how to talk their language. I want you to leave and go back to your quarters. Don't you worry about me. If anything happens, just ship my body home." He gave them all a hug and pat on the back and off the elders trudged into the darkness.

Alone, Golden went to the stream and yelled, "We're finished over here. Do you know who we are?"

Fifty Klansmen yelled back, "You're those

blankety-blank Mormons, and we're here to teach you a lesson! We warned you to git out of our county!'

Golden said, 'Yes, we're Mormons. And let me tell you something — Mormons have horns. You cross that stream, we'll gore the hell right out of you!"

Golden heard a noise behind him. He turned and saw ... the elders had come back! They were standing in a line just behind him.

By the light of the moon the Klan couldn't tell whether they had horns or not. One by one they got on their horses and rode off. The tar was dumped on the ground, the cauldron put back on the wagon and the rest left without ruffling a single hair on a Mormon head.

One of the elders later wrote to Golden how one grand wizard told another, "By the light of a full moon, the Mormons grow horns and become vicious. They should be left alone."

GENERAL AUTHORITY

In 1892, Golden was made one of the Seven Presidents of the Seventies, a high Church position where he rubbed shoulders with the First Presidency and the Council of the Twelve. Like all General Authorities, he was given assignments to travel throughout the Church, speaking and inspiring the Saints to live more righteously. As a seventy, he had special responsibility over the Church's missionary program.

RE(ve)LATION

Golden was under no illusions about deserving his calling. He often said that in his case, "If it isn't inspiration or revelation, then it's relation. If Heber C. Kimball wasn't my father, I wouldn't be a damn thing in this Church."

PRAISE THE LORD
AND PASS
THE SIX-SHOOTER

Whenever a problem came up that required a man with a few more rough edges than the usual General Authority possessed, J. Golden was the man called to deal with it.

He sometimes commented that the other brethren viewed him as "God's gunslinger."

SEAT OF REASON

A stake president in Wyoming wrote asking for a General Authority. The young men were going around with pistols in their hip pockets and shooting them off after basketball games and dances. There was going to be a killing if somebody didn't talk to them.

So President Grant called Golden and said, "This sounds like an assignment for you, Brother Kimball."

Golden protested, "Why me?"

The President said, "Well, you're the only cowboy that's a General Authority. They'll listen to you!"

So Uncle Golden went to Wyoming. He wrote the stake president and asked him to gather all the youth into the largest hall they had. The stake president was happy to oblige. When the time came, they were all there. The doors were even locked so the youth couldn't get out.

The troublemakers were yahooing, firing off pistols and throwing paper airplanes and showing no respect for Brother Kimball when he arrived. Golden took all this in and thought the direct approach best.

"Go to Hell!" He said.

The auditorium suddenly became still.

He said it again, "Go to Hell!"

You could hear a pin drop. All eyes were riveted on the angry scarecrow at the podium. Having grabbed their attention, Golden forged ahead. "That's where you're all going to go if you don't change your ways! I hear some of you have been walking around town with pistols in your hip pockets. Better be careful — might go off and blow your brains out!"

And he walked out of the hall. The roughnecks were left with their mouths hanging open.

Later, the stake president wrote to say the rowdies were better behaved after learning where their seat of reason was.

PERIODIC PRODIGALS

Golden understood the wilder impulses of youth, having been rather unruly himself.

The young men and women in Fillmore were going through various phases of wildness and obedience. This was kind of a cyclical thing, depending on whom they were looking up to, and who was in charge and what kind of examples they were following. Golden was called and asked to speak to these periodical prodigals.

The conference was held in a large room with a stage up front where all the dignitaries sat.

Speaker after straight-laced speaker browbeat the youth for their insolence, sin and lack of respect. Once they had spoken, they left the podium and sat down on the front row of the chapel. Golden was left all alone on the stand.

He slowly arose, his thumbs in his vest pocket. Sticking out his chest, he said, "Brothers and Sisters, you don't need to worry about these young people — they'll take care of themselves. It's these old bald-headed bastards on the front row you want to look out for."

The room erupted. Never has a Fillmore church hall heard such laughter, before or since.

MISSIONARY TRAINING

Working with a stake president, Golden finally persuaded one of the wildest, roughest young men in town to go on a mission. A party was held for him the night before his farewell.

Golden decided to attend and discovered it turned out to be a rather raucous affair. There was dancing and a considerable amount of drinking. The crowd wanted the new young missionary to stand up and say a few words.

He appeared to be drunker than anyone else. The young elder staggered to the stage, slurred out a few sentences and told his girlfriend he'd be back in a couple of months. He then slipped off the stage and fell dead drunk to the floor.

Golden took the bishop aside. "I think you ought

to keep him around here for a little while longer and kick him in the ass every day. Then he might turn out to be a good elder."

WHALE OF A TALE

Certain people loved to hear Golden speak. Sometimes they'd even follow him from conference to conference. Golden reasoned that all of the sodbusters and cowboys and nuts in the Church could relate to him, while all the educated and well-to-do members could relate to Heber J. Grant, because he was more polished.

Golden was happy to divide things up that way. He always felt he had a lot more interesting experiences than Heber.

While in Kanab for a conference, Golden delivered his usual talk but his eye kept straying to a certain man on the back row, and he thought, "He's my kind of guy. He's going to come up and talk to me, I know he is." Sure enough, when the meeting was over, he came up. Golden knew he was his kind of man because all he had on was a loincloth and moccasins and a long beard.

After the talk the man patiently waited for the crowd around Golden to thin before he stepped forward and put his hand out and said, "Brother Kimball, I'm not active in the Church."

Golden looked at the man's unusual attire. "I gathered that. What's your problem?"

He said, "Well, it's very simple. My problem is I don't believe the Old Testament to be the word of God. I don't believe Jonah could live in the belly of a whale for three days."

Golden said, "That's one hell of a reason for not being active. That's enough to take me out of activity, I tell you." But the man was very serious and didn't understand Golden's good-natured ribbing.

So Golden sighed and said, "Look, I'll make you a deal. I'm soon going to die and I'll get over on the other side and I'll look up Jonah and find out how the hell he did it. You stay active until I get back." The man thought it over and said, "It's a deal." They shook hands on it.

Golden was informed later by the bishop that the man became active and was teaching Sunday School. He even gave up his loincloth for a suit.

GOD'S WILL

A woman came up to Golden after a meeting with one of the toughest Gospel questions he ever faced. She was a sweet and lovely sister.

"Brother Kimball, I've got a real problem. You've got to help me. I have two older brothers. The older of the two was out haying last August and was hit by lightning as he stood in his wagon. At dusk the horses brought him back in the wagon to the corral and he was dead. He was just as fine a man as God ever created, Brother Kimball. He was the bishop and he taught at school and he was a great father and husband and was active in the community. The whole town came to his funeral."

Brother Kimball expressed his sincere regret. She said, "Well, that's not my problem. I miss him but I know I'll see him again. It's my younger brother. He's no good at all. He smokes, he drinks, he gambles, he cheats on his wife. He's a terrible father and husband, and he's still alive. I can't figure it out. Why would the Lord take the good one?"

She started to cry. Golden put his arm around her and said, "Oh, Sister, now there's got to be an answer here."

He prayed, but nothing came to him. He prayed again very hard for several minutes. Finally, he felt inspired. "Sister," he said, "do you know what it is? It's God's will. God doesn't want that jackass brother of yours any more than you do."

The good sister went away happy with this answer.

FASTING AND BRAYING

Golden was speaking in eastern Utah in a conference. The stake president took him aside and said, "In the afternoon session, there's going to be some people that aren't active in the Church. We call them 'Latter-day Ain'ts' and they may make some catcalls and have some fun with you." Golden said, "Oh, that doesn't bother me."

Sure enough, when he got up to speak, they yelled out, "We can't hear you up here." Golden stopped, looked at them, and returned to his address. They yelled again, "We still can't hear you up here."

He stopped and looked at them again and this time said, "You know, that's the way it's going to be on the morning of the first resurrection — a bunch of jackasses like you will be over in some corner telling Jesus, 'We can't hear you over here!'"

QUICK AND THE DEAD

President Grant sent a note to Golden. The note read that there was a member of the stake presidency from Coalville, who had passed away. His wife had requested Golden speak at the funeral.

Golden didn't get the note until he returned from a Church assignment in Southern California. By then the funeral was in an hour and Coalville was almost two hours away.

He hopped in his Model T and drove as fast as he could. When he arrived, the funeral was almost over. The bishop saw Golden walk in. "Brother Kimball, come forward. We'd like to hear from you."

He went up and said, "I'm very happy to be here. I'm sorry I'm late. I want to tell you what a wonderful person this man was. I knew him, I've stayed in his home. He was an inspiration to me. He was a good father, he was a good husband. He goes to a great reward ..."

As he started to hit his stride, he looked out in the audience. About the eighth row back, there sat the man he thought was dead!

So he looked down in the casket. He did not recognize the man lying there. Confused, he turned and said, "Say, Bishop, who the hell's dead around here anyway?"

A REALLY
EFFECTIVE DUNKING

Uncle Golden liked to keep track of the members of the Church, especially down Highway 89.

He tried to show up and speak at baptisms, funerals and weddings. The growth of the Church and the members' private lives meant a great deal to him.

Periodically he would go back and inquire how some person was doing.

In Salina, he went to a bishopric meeting and asked, "I'm curious to know about Brother Nichols. Whatever happened to Brother Nichols?"

The bishop said, "I'm sorry to tell you this, Brother Kimball, but he's fallen back into his old ways. He was baptized and came out to the meetings for a long time, but now he's chasing women and drinking and smoking. He is not living the gospel teachings."

Golden said, "I'm sorry to hear that. Who was it

that baptized him?"

The surprised bishop gently reminded Golden, "Brother Kimball, you did — you were the one who baptized him."

"I did?" Golden exclaimed, "I'm really sorry about that."

"Oh, Brother Kimball, it's not your fault that he's fallen away."

"That's not what I'm sorry about. I'm sorry I didn't keep the son of a bitch under the water longer!"

DEAD AGAIN

Against his wishes, Golden was once asked to talk about genealogy, a topic he had no feeling for. He got up and said, "They want me to talk about genealogy. As far as I'm concerned, it's work for the dead done by the half dead." Then he sat down.

HAT IN HAND

Lightning hit a barn in Nevada and completely destroyed both it and all the animals. The brother who owned the barn was left destitute. President Grant called on Golden to go out and organize some relief for this good brother. Unbeknownst to Golden, the neighbors in the Elko area had already taken up a collection.

When he arrived, he called a special meeting of the members. When they were assembled, Golden took off his cowboy hat and said, "I think we all ought to delve into our pockets and help this brother out because of his desperate situation." The hat went around the room and came back to Golden empty.

Back in Salt Lake his secretary asked, "How did the fund-raising meeting go?" Golden responded, "I was just grateful to get my hat back!"

SEVENTIES GIVE 110%

Golden felt very strongly about the callings of the seventies. He maintained they did all of the hard missionary work for the Church while the high priests only sat around and gassed about obscure points of doctrine.

In an Ogden stake he addressed a group of men before setting them apart as seventies. "I want you brethren to be dedicated and hard-working seventies in the service of the Lord. If I find out you're not, the next time I'm up here, I'll release all of you and make you high priests."

GOING SEVENTY

A brother was called to be a seventy. As was customary back then, he and several others went to the Church headquarters to be set apart by a General Authority.

In this case the responsibility fell to J. Golden Kimball.

The good brother was not sure what this new calling entailed. When it was his turn to be set apart, he asked Brother Golden to tell him what was involved in the calling of a seventy.

"One hell of a lot. Now let's get on with it!"

SLIVER OF CONTENTION

Spring City had a bishop who was a very mild, reserved, gentlemanly kind of fellow. The Relief Society president, however, was a different story.

Sister Brown was essentially running the ward. She was telling the bishop who was paying a full tithing and who should be called on missions, what young men shouldn't be going because they were fornicators and smoked, and who should not be called to serve in the Sunday School because they had never returned the tools they had borrowed from their neighbor.

Several members of the ward could see the poor bishop was in over his head. They wrote to

President Grant, begging him to send somebody to fix their problem.

President Grant sent Golden.

When Golden arrived, he interviewed both the bishop and Sister Brown. He then asked for just a few minutes in sacrament meeting.

At the close of the meeting Golden was called to speak. "I want to ask you all a question. Would you please show by the raise of hands: How many of you have ever had a sliver in your ass?"

One little girl who'd recently gotten one going down a slippery slide raised her hand. Slowly other people started raising theirs.

"Good — you know you need somebody else to help you take it out. You can't do it by yourself. Well, that's why I'm here. You have a sliver in your ass, brothers and sisters, and I'm here to help you take it out.

"Now, all who can release Sister Brown as the Relief Society president, would you do so by the usual sign? Are there any opposed? Good. Thank you."

GOD KNOWS

Golden went to a ward in the Avenues in Salt Lake City to set a certain brother apart. The man was a Central European who had recently been converted to the Church. He had a most peculiar name: Ivanovich Ignatovicious

Since the first thing one does in setting anyone apart is give their name, Golden put his hands on the brother's head and asked, "What is your name?"

The brother responded, "My name is Ivanovich Ignatovicious."

Golden said, "Thank you very much. Ivano ... Ignato ... what was that name again? Could you repeat it for me one more time?"

"Ivanovich Ignatovicious," he repeated. Golden said, "Thank you very much. Ivan ... Ivan ... One more time, brother."

The name was repeated again and again. Golden tried to repeat it but failed. He then paused and said, "Oh, hell, the Lord knows who you are," and went on with the ordination.

MAE WEST

All kinds of stories followed Uncle Golden
around the Church. Some were true, others were
embroidered truths, and still others were spun
out of whole cloth.

A nephew once asked him if he'd heard the
latest J. Golden Kimball story. "No," he said,
"and I don't want to hear it. Things that happen
now are either blamed on me or Mae West."

Golden's
Straight Men

Early in the century it was Church policy for General Authorities to travel in pairs, when possible, to discharge their assignments. Some of the funniest stories have to do with the unusual pairing of J. Golden with these unwitting "straight men."

NOT WHAT
YOU SAY ...

"When I speak, I don't try to be funny. When the brethren say something, the people are inspired. I can say the same thing, and everybody laughs.

"I went to Logan with Melvin J. Ballard, one of the great orators of the Church. We were to speak at a stake conference. Elder Ballard was first. He stood and said, 'Brothers and Sisters, the Lord alone knows what I'm going to say ...' Then he went on and gave a wonderful talk.

"I thought, 'I can do that.' So I stood up and said, 'Brothers and Sisters, God only knows what I'm going to say ...' and they all laughed!"

LOVE THY NEIGHBOR

J. Golden Kimball had this to say about his fellow General Authorities. "I love them all. But I love some a hell of lot more than I do others."

OF MICE AND BORING MEN

J. Golden did not relish meetings for meetings' sake. He once characterized the excessive minutiae involved in meetings with Church officials as "Sweeping up mice turds."

GIVE, SAID THE LITTLE STREAM

Years ago the Church had a policy that every stake, when possible, should have a farm or ranch. Because Uncle Golden had been a cowboy, rancher and farmer, he was asked to go out and look at land being considered by the stakes. One such request came in the summer of 1934 from President Grant, who wanted Golden to go down and look at a ranch near Manti.

Golden drove down. The stake presidency showed him the piece of ground. He walked around and made several notes. A week later he gave a positive report at the welfare meeting conducted by President Grant and recommended that the Church make the purchase.

President Grant then said, "Brother Kimball, was there any water on it?" Golden said, "Oh, yes, there's a small stream that runs down the south fence line." President Grant said, "How big was it?" He said, "Well, it wasn't much of a stream at all. Maybe one or two second feet."

The President, who wasn't a farmer or rancher and didn't understand the terminology, said, "I don't understand. How big was it?" Golden paused and said, "Well, Heber, I could piss about halfway across it." President Grant said immediately, "Brother Kimball, you're out of order!" Golden responded, "Yes, and if I weren't out of order I could have pissed all the way across it."

RANK HAS ITS PRIVILEGES

"I have often been assigned to speak in St. George, but I am assigned to go there in either July or August. Heber goes down in January or February, but that's because he's the prophet."

SINGING PROPHET

Golden was attending a conference in St. George at the Tabernacle with President Grant. By this time, Golden's stories and language had become so offensive to President Grant that he demanded that Golden travel with him.

On this particular occasion, the president chose to speak from a favorite text of his which was, "That which we persist in doing, not that the nature of the thing changes, but our ability to overcome it is increased."

He cited as an example his inability to sing as a young man, and the difficulty he encountered and how he practiced and practiced and took lessons, and finally developed an acceptable singing voice. To prove his point, he sang one verse from one of his favorite patriotic hymns, *The Flag Without a Stain*. He then sat down.

Golden then stood before the congregation. He cleared his high-pitched voice and said, "Brothers and Sisters, I have to admire Heber's ability to persist and overcome his limitations. But after listening to him sing, I still think he sounds like hell."

ZZZZZZZZZ

Francis M. Lyman, a member of the Quorum of the Twelve, would pick either B. H. Roberts or Uncle Golden as traveling companions. Francis

Lyman was given to speaking at great, sometimes excessive, length. It drove both Brother Roberts and Uncle Golden crazy, so they attempted to pass off the assignment between them.

Golden recorded in his diary how he would get even with Brother Lyman for talking too much by snoring all night. Golden felt they canceled each other out. But Golden found that Brother Lyman was very bothered by his snoring because he couldn't get a good night's sleep.

Brother Lyman one night awakened Golden and said, "I was wondering ... It's your snoring again. I can't sleep. Would you mind closing your mouth in the night so I can get some sleep?"

Uncle Golden leaned up on his pillow and said, "I'll make you a deal, Francis: I'll close it at night if you'll close it in the daytime."

— Attributed to President
Spencer W. Kimball

CALLED OF GOD

There is only one man in the history of the Mormon Church who was a United States senator and an apostle of the Lord at the same time, and that was Reed Smoot.

Despite the fact that Reed was a Republican and Golden a confirmed Democrat, the two men liked each other. There was a kind of pleasant repartee between the two of them.

When Smoot was made a member of the Quorum of the Twelve, Golden ran into him in the old church office building and said, "I understand they've made you an apostle of the Lord now."

Smoot said, "Yes, they have."

Golden patted the newly minted apostle on the back and said, "You were truly called of God, Reed, because nobody else would have thought of you."

MAY/DECEMBER
ROMANCE

Reed Smoot was a widower. In Washington, D.C., he met Alice Sheets, fell in love and they decided to marry.

There was a considerable difference, however, in their ages.

Brother Smoot returned to Salt Lake to ask the brethren for their approval. They said, "Oh, yes, she will be wonderful. She will be a great companion for you."

Smoot was leaving the meeting when he met
Golden on the front steps of Church
headquarters.

The groom-to-be said, "I guess you've heard
about my plans to remarry."

Golden said, "Congratulations. But you know,
Reed, you and I are old men. And Sister Sheets,
well, she's a young woman. I don't know,
Reed... I think on the wedding night she's going
to expect just a little bit more than the laying on
of hands."

WRONG GUY

Rudger Clawson was the president of the
Quorum of the Twelve, and would have become
the prophet had he outlived Heber J. Grant.
Golden was often assigned to travel with
Rudger.

This was a difficult situation for Uncle Golden.
Rudger was a man with a very limited sense of
humor. In most of his talks, he told the same
story about his tragic missionary experience in

Georgia, on the 21st of July 1877.

Rudger and his companion, Joseph Standing, were tracting when a dozen men surrounded them and said, "We're going to take you into the woods and beat you." Elder Standing foolishly resisted and was shot in the face and died.

The leader of the mob said, "Shoot the other one!" Elder Clawson folded his arms and said, "Go ahead and shoot." This unnerved the gang and they rode off.

This became a great epic moment in Rudger's life and he would tell this story, time and time again. As Rudger grew older, the story became embellished. And longer.

When Golden went with Rudger to conferences, he seldom spoke, because Rudger took all the time telling his story. Golden would travel all the way to California, Texas or New York just to give the closing prayer.

After one such meeting, a man caught up to Golden and said, "I'm sorry we didn't get to hear from you. We have come so far to hear you speak and we're very disappointed."

The man then asked, "Brother Kimball, aren't

you getting just a little bit tired of hearing the same story, over and over again?"

"Yes, I am. And the more I think about it, I feel they shot the wrong man."

OLD YELLER

Golden's office in the Church headquarters was on the second floor. He was only a few offices removed from Elder Rudger Clawson.

As Elder Clawson's hearing declined with age, Golden's patience with Rudger's phone conversations similarly waned. On one particularly trying occasion, Rudger was yelling out his request to a caller for a piece of information he required.

The bellowing between the two went on for

some time. Golden endured this as long as he could. Finally, he walked down the hall, opened Rudger's office door and said, "Ah, hell, Rudger, write him a letter!"

MERCIFUL LORD

Rudger Clawson never became prophet. Golden said it was just as well. "I would have been the death of him. I damn near killed Heber."

SWEARING

J. Golden's swearing, picked up during his years as a cowboy, was legendary. It provides grist for some of the most, um, "colorful" stories that Mormons give themselves permission to tell. He peppered his speech with "hells" and "damns" — which, any cowboy will tell you, isn't really swearing.

ELDER DOLITTLE

"I am sorry about my swearing, but it is the only language animals understand. Mules and horses never respond unless you swear at them."

NIGHTMARES

Sister Clarissa Williams, the president of the Relief Society, was a very prim and proper woman. She also wasn't afraid to speak her mind. So it was with justifiable trepidation when Golden saw her approach him on the street one day.

"Brother Kimball, you're an embarrassment to the Church."

He allowed that she might be right.

The good sister persisted. She went on to offer some sisterly counsel, "All you'd have to do is stop swearing and act more like one of the Lord's anointed."

He said he'd give it some thought.

She said, "You are one of the Lord's anointed, aren't you?"

He said that was the general consensus.

"You've certainly received some revelation, haven't you?"

Golden's patience had run out. "No, but I've had some damn good nightmares!" he snapped.

STOP THAT #!&*!

A stake president took Uncle Golden aside down in Salina, and said, "Brother Kimball, you've got to talk to the youth. I can't send them on missions, they're swearing too much!"

Golden wasn't sure he'd heard right. "You want me to talk to them?" The stake president explained that they might listen to someone who spoke their language, so to speak.

So Golden gathered them all together and said, "I understand you brethren are not going to be called on missions unless you can give up your swearing. You can do it. Hell, I did."

GOLDEN'S CALF

J. Golden, dressed and ready for church, was out feeding the calf. The calf shook his head and threw milk all over Golden's new suit.

He looked down at his suit and said, "If I had my way, and if I weren't a General Authority of

the Mormon Church, I'd shove your head right
to the bottom of this damn bucket!"

IN THE HEAT
OF PASSION

A sister once asked Golden, "Why do you swear
so much? President Grant doesn't swear. Have
you ever heard President Grant swear in all your
life?"

The sister looked very surprised when he said,
yes, he had. "What do you mean?" she
demanded, unwilling to believe any such thing.

Golden told her this story to prove he was right:

"President Grant and I were down in St. George
one summer. It hadn't rained for months. On our
way out of St. George to Cedar City we stopped.
All over the valley we saw the simmering heat,
the withering crops and the dying cattle.

"Finally, I said, 'Look at that, Heber.'

"He said, 'Yes, look at it.'

"And I said, 'It's a damn shame, isn't it!'

"And he said, 'Yes, it is.'"

YOU THINK I'M BAD....

YOU SHOULD HEAR PRESIDENT GRANT!

TRAVELING MAN

President Grant gave Golden an ultimatum on his swearing. "If you continue, you will have to travel with either Rudger Clawson or me."

Golden always said, "It's that damn contraption, the telephone, that gets me in trouble, because before it was invented I could go out and say anything I wanted to and then I'd get back and deny it. But now they call back and tell Heber

what I've said and he's waiting for me at the
train station.

"He always says the same thing: 'Did you say
that?' I always say the same thing: 'Yes I did.'

"Heber then instructs me, 'Get back on the train
and go apologize.'

"I've been doing a lot of traveling lately."

WYOMINGESE
FOR "HELLO"

Golden once went to Wyoming and got a little
carried away. He said some things that, on
serious reflection, he wished hadn't been
reported back to the president of the Church.

When he got back, President Grant called him in
and said, "I've warned you. I've told you. And
now I got this phone call, and you cursed these
people. You cussed at them and we can't have
that. You're traveling with me from now on."

Golden thought a moment. "Wait a minute,

Heber — you've got to remember, that's Wyoming. It's pretty bleak up there. It's pretty drab. The winters are long. Life is hard. If you don't call them sons of bitches when you speak to them, they don't hardly feel welcomed."

LIES, DAMN LIES, AND WHAT YOU READ IN THE PAPER

Golden was assigned to go to speak in Las Vegas. He was told by the stake president that there were some newspaper reporters in the audience. They had heard he was often given to swearing when he preached and they would have loved to catch him in some of his more colorful remarks for their papers.

Golden got up to speak. He acknowledged their presence by saying, "Now over here on the front row sit a number of newspaper reporters. They're waiting for me to swear because they want to put in their articles that I am a swearing elder.

"If they do that, they're damn liars."

OH, FOR
HECK'S SAKE!

In Cedar City they were going to broadcast a
meeting of the Saints that included two cities to
the south, St. George and Las Vegas. President
Grant was concerned with Golden's language
because the FCC could remove the Church's
license to broadcast if Golden used profanity.

President Grant called Golden and said, "Golden, I've prepared some notes for you. This is going to be the talk you're going to give when you go with me to Cedar City. Do you understand?"

Golden said, "Well, I'll do my best." So they drove down to Cedar City.

As the broadcast began, President Grant was the first to speak. He gave a fine, dignified speech. He then introduced Uncle Golden. Golden arose and took the prepared speech out of his pocket. "Dear Brothers and Sisters, it is a great ... uh, uh ... privilege to ... uh, uh ... be with you ... uh, uh, uh ... today."

He stumbled along for a few more lines and finally stopped and said, "Hell, Heber, I can't read this damn thing!"

WORD OF WISDOM

Early in the Church, the Word of Wisdom was not practiced as, shall we say, "religiously" as it is today. One could indulge in a little tea, or coffee, and still be a faithful, active member with a clear conscience. President Heber J. Grant in the 1930s changed all that. He made adherence to the Word of Wisdom a hallmark of the restored Church.

Golden loved a good cup of coffee and struggled with this new requirement with courage, determination — and very little success.

QUIT WHEN
I'M DEAD

When President Heber J. Grant said the Church was going to observe the Word of Wisdom and that the 89th Section was going to be enforced, Golden went in to him and said, "Heber, you can't do this to me. I've been drinking coffee all my life. What am I supposed to do?" President Grant said, "Well, Brother Kimball, try your very best to give it up."

The year before Golden died, he gave a talk at stake conference. "I want you Brothers and Sisters to know that I observe the Word of Wisdom. I still have a little bit of a problem, but I've just about got it licked. I'm 85 years old and I've just about got it licked."

COFFEE MUG

This was an incident that took place in Keely's Restaurant, an old diner in downtown Salt Lake frequented by Uncle Golden.

Golden walked in and ordered a cup of coffee. They brought it to him and he went to a back booth to sip it.

While he was sitting enjoying his drink, a woman came by on her way to the ladies room. She stopped, came back and peered closely at Golden. "Aren't you J. Golden Kimball of the First Council of Seventy?" She probed, "And isn't that coffee you're drinking?"

He looked at her for a moment and said, "Sister, you're the third woman today to mistake me for that old son of a bitch."

GOOD INTENTIONS

They had a luncheon honoring Uncle Golden at the old Rotisserie Restaurant on Main Street. All the business people from downtown — Jews and Gentiles, professional people and professors — were there.

Golden was seated at the head table. When the waiter came up to him and said, "What would you like to drink, Brother Kimball?" Golden paused, looked around, and then said, "Water. I'd like water to drink."

The waiter then turned to the man next to Golden, a doctor, to take his order. The doctor knew Golden fairly well and said to the waiter, "I'd like coffee and, by the way, would you bring Brother Kimball a cup, too. He likes coffee."

Golden's eyes drifted to the ceiling and he said loud enough so everyone could hear, "The Lord heard me say 'water.'"

HOT CHOCOLATE
WITH A TWIST

The prophet once asked Golden to take the new Deseret Sunday school president up to the Brigham City conference. "His name is David O. McKay. He just got back from the Scottish mission." Golden agreed to escort the nice, young fellow.

It was winter. They traveled all day and night by sled in the bitter cold. Finally, they arrived with an hour to spare before the meeting.

Golden thought he was going to die. He reasoned he needed a coffee — bad. So he innocently suggested they go over to the Idle Isle Restaurant for breakfast.

The aroma of hot coffee filled the little diner. When the waitress asked the two gentlemen what they'd like, Brother McKay said, "Some ham and eggs and two cups of hot chocolate, please."

Golden excused himself and found the waitress who had taken their order. "Would you mind putting a little coffee in my hot chocolate, please?" he asked. She said that would be OK, they did it all the time up there.

The waitress came by a minute later with two steaming mugs and said, "Now, which one of you wanted coffee in your hot chocolate?"

Caught, Golden said, "Ah, hell, put it in both of them."

Brother McKay laughed uncontrollably.

GROUNDS
FOR A STORY

To Golden's chagrin, young Brother McKay told everybody the story at the conference. And he kept on doing it every time he spoke.

"I wish he'd keep his damn mouth shut," he reportedly groused. "Maybe Heber will release him and we won't hear any more about him!"

IS THAT A CIGAR
IN YOUR POCKET?

Golden attended a stake conference in the
Cottonwood area. The first order of business
was to set apart the new seventies. A chair was
set up in front for this purpose.

It went without a hitch — until the last man. As
the man sat, Uncle Golden leaned over to ask
his name. He saw a cigar in the man's inside suit
coat pocket.

He thought this was unusual for a new seventy,
but went ahead. In the setting apart, he said,
"By the power vested in me, I ordain you a
seventy in The Church of Jesus Christ of
Latter-day Saints, cigar and all!"
The baffled murmur in the meetinghouse
showed the crowd's puzzlement. Kimball had
the new seventy stand up and take the cigar out

of his pocket and explain to all of them what it was doing there.

The man sheepishly told how on the previous Friday at his office somebody had come in and said, "I'm a new father!" passing out Cuban cigars to everyone. "I took one," he said, "and put it in my upper left-hand pocket and forgot about it. I only own one suit and I put it on to come to this meeting."

COMMITTING COFFEE

Another time he was in Walgreens drugstore. He sat down at the far end of the long counter. After he was served a cup of coffee, a man walked by, turned and looked at him and what he was drinking. "Aren't you J. Golden Kimball?" the man demanded.

Golden sighed and answered, "Yes, I am."

The man straightened up and said, "I'd rather commit adultery than drink coffee!"

Golden responded, "Hell, who wouldn't?"

ELEVATED THOUGHT

Golden's nephew, Ranch Kimball, sometimes picked his uncle up at noon on beautiful, sunny days outside the old Church administration building. He'd take his favorite relative up City Creek Canyon for a cup of coffee and a sandwich.

One day they were sitting near the top of City Creek Canyon enjoying a pot of coffee over a small fire. Ranch asked, "Uncle Golden, does it bother you being a General Authority who drinks coffee?"

Golden thought for a minute and said, "Hell, no, it doesn't bother me at all. The 89th Section doesn't apply at this altitude."

GOOD FOR WHAT AILS YOU

Once Uncle Golden accompanied a train full of General Authorities to create the first stake in Denver, Colorado. On the return journey he was very ill with the flu. When he boarded the train, he said he just wanted to go to bed. But President Grant insisted. "Oh, Golden, come down and join us for dinner."

The waiter came to Uncle Golden and asked what he would like to order. "Nothing for me. I think I'm coming down with the flu."

The waiter said, "Sir, I know how to lick the flu — I get a big, tall glass and I fill it halfway with whiskey and the rest with coffee. You drink that down and go back to your berth and sleep through the night. When we get to Salt Lake tomorrow morning, you'll feel just fine."

There was a deathly silence in the diner. President Grant and all the brethren waited anxiously for Golden's response. He looked around at everyone and loudly said, "I'll have to pass on that, brother, that's very kind of you, but I'll have to pass."

The waiter moved on. He was just about to go through the swinging door to the kitchen when Golden stood up and yelled, "Oh, waiter, waiter! About that drink you suggested ... You couldn't make that half Postum, could you?"

YOUR FLU MEDICINE, SIR.

CLASSIC GOLDEN

Everyone has their favorite J. Golden story. The stories people choose to tell probably say more about the teller of the story than it does about Uncle Golden. He is the shoot-from-the-lip gospel gunslinger that we all secretly wish we had the wit, courage, and spiritual self-assurance to be.

GRAND OLD
PARTY POOPER

Golden was scheduled to speak at the Tabernacle but showed up at the Assembly Hall (the building just south of the Tabernacle on Temple Square) by mistake. He unwittingly walked in on a big meeting of Utah Republicans.

Senator (and Apostle) Reed Smoot was conducting. He knew that Golden wasn't a Republican but a good Democrat. The senator thought he'd have a little fun with his fellow General Authority. Smoot brought the gavel down on the podium.

"We're very happy to welcome all of you here to this Republican state convention. We're especially delighted to see Brother J. Golden Kimball of the First Council of Seventy. This represents a change in his political affiliation. Would you give the opening prayer, Brother Kimball?"

Realizing his mistake, Golden jumped up like he'd been shot. "I'll pass on that, Reed. I'd just as soon the Lord didn't know I was here."

LORD'S ANOINTED

The most famous story that everyone seems to know about Uncle Golden relates to his crossing Main Street on his way over to the Salt Lake Temple from the southwest corner of the Hotel Utah.

Some reckless youths came west on South

Temple in a speeding jalopy and turned abruptly around the corner without stopping. They barely missed Golden, spattering his trousers with mud.

He shook his cane at them, "You sons of perdition! Have you no respect for the priesthood? Can't you tell the difference between a common gentile and one of the Lord's anointed?"

HOLEY HAT TRICK!

Golden went in to buy a new Stetson hat at ZCMI. He loved Stetson hats. He walked up to the counter and said, "I'd like to look at that Stetson hat right over there. I've had my eye on it for several weeks."

The salesman brought it over, dusted it off and said, "This is our very best Stetson."
Uncle Golden said, "Well, how much is it?"

"Sixty-five dollars."

"Sixty-five dollars!" Golden exclaimed. He

looked the hat over critically and said, "Where are the holes?"

"Holes?" the man asked, puzzled, "There are no holes in Stetson hats. Why should they have holes?"

"Holes for the ears of the jackass that would pay $65 for it."

RESPECT FOR NOAH

Uncle Golden had retained a small portion of his ranch in Round Valley. He loved to go there often. My father, Noble Kimball, drove him up on several occasions.

The big problem, according to my father, was getting a team of mules hitched up. Some stake in that area had given him a pair of mules that refused to work together. They were, as expected, very stubborn. My Dad said sometimes it would take most of the morning to get the mules hitched.

On this occasion, Golden and Dad succeeded in getting one mule out of the barn and hitched up. The other mule could see what was on their minds, so as they led him out, he reared and ripped the rope away from my father and took off in a run down the road.

The first mule, seeing that the second mule had run off, did the same thing. In the process, he tipped over the wagon and the tongue broke off the wagon. Both mules headed off in different directions at a full gallop.

The two men stood and watched in silence. Finally, my father said Golden took off his hat and threw it on the ground. "You know, Noble, there's something I'll never be able to figure out: How Noah got two of those sons of bitches on the ark!"

TROLLEY SQUIRE

Golden's favorite Christmas story about himself went as follows:

On a snowy day two weeks before Christmas, he was crossing South Temple to the north door of ZCMI. He walked slowly to the middle of the ice-slick street.

A woman burst out of the north door of ZCMI with a pile of packages in her hands and no clear line of sight.

She plowed right into Golden.

Packages flew everywhere. Golden was knocked down and the woman fell on top of him. Together they began to slide south towards the curb.

All the traffic stopped. Everyone stood entranced by this most unlikely scene.

They slid until they hit the curb. It was then the woman realized someone was beneath her. She brushed the snow away and exclaimed, "Oh, Brother Kimball, it's you! Speak to me! Are you all right?"

"It's all right, Sister, but you'll have to get off here. This is as far as I go," he painfully croaked.

IT CAN ONLY GET BETTER

Golden sometimes visited the members in Delta, located in the harsh West Desert of Utah.

He always came back grateful.

"As far as I'm concerned, God's creative juices ran out on him when he got to Delta. Delta is not the end of the earth, but it's just slightly beyond Delta, about over by the Nevada border.

"Every time I go down there I tell them the same thing and they all laugh. I say, 'Brothers and Sisters, you do not have to fear Hell. You are living in it!'"

COOL ADVICE

On one occasion Golden was in St. George attending stake conference. It was a long meeting, and a very hot day, about 118 degrees.

Golden was the last to speak. At the podium he looked at those poor people out there in the audience: the women wilting in those full skirts and bonnets, and the men, tan from half their foreheads down, in black suits bravely perspiring.

He told them, "I do not know how you do it, Brothers and Sisters. This insufferable heat, the Indians, the scorpions, the flooding Virgin River. I don't know how you do it. If I had a house in St. George and I had a house in Hell, I'd rent out the one in St. George and move straight to Hell."

SORRY. SORTA.

Some saints in St. George reported that they were insulted by the "rather live in Hell" comment. President Grant said, "You've got to go back down and apologize to those people for what you've said."

He did as he was told. Kind of.

In a packed meeting of Dixie saints eager to hear his apology, Golden said, "President Grant said I've got to apologize to you because I said if I had a home in St. George and one in Hell, I'd sell the one in St. George and go to Hell.

"I'm apologizing, but it's still the truth."

LONG JOHN

On one of his assignments, Golden stayed at the home of the local bishop. In the morning, Golden found he needed a toilet and he needed it bad.

So he asked, "Bishop, where do you go?"

"Oh," the man said, "You go down through the orchard about 100 yards, take a left, and you'll see the place."

Golden peered down the direction indicated and said, "Hell, you need to pack a lunch!"

SUFFER BY COMPARISON

It was Easter and Golden had been asked to give the Easter sermon at the LDS institute in Logan.

When Golden got up to speak, he noticed a beautiful arrangement of Easter lilies on one corner of the pulpit. He looked at the bouquet and then at the congregation and then back again at the bouquet. Before saying a word, he picked up the bouquet, walked across the stand and placed it on the piano.

When he came back, he said in his high-pitched voice, "The contrast was too great."

NON-MURDER MOST FOWL

Once Golden drove out to Stansbury to get a turkey for Thanksgiving. He gave it to his wife, Jennie, to prepare for the big traditional family gathering.

When the day came, he sat down all set for a turkey dinner. To his great surprise, his wife served a roast of beef.

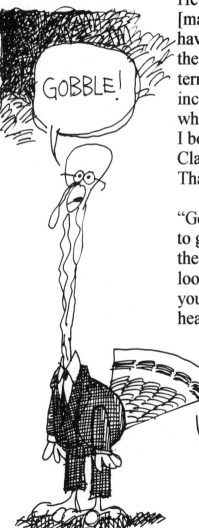

GOBBLE!

MOTHER! HAVE YOU DRESSED THE TURKEY?

He said to her, "Mother [many Kimball men have traditionally called their wives this as a term of endearment, including Golden], where's that turkey that I bought out at Brother Clark's farm for Thanksgiving?"

"Golden, when I went to get it ready to cook, the long, scrawny neck looked so much like yours, I didn't have the heart to cook it."

NO OPTIONS

Some important dignitaries arrived in Salt Lake City. President Grant called J. Golden and said, "I need someone to show them around the city."

Golden hated these assignments. "Oh, Heber, you know how I am with my cowboy vocabulary. I don't want to embarrass the Church. I'd prefer if you'd ask someone else."

Heber impatiently replied, "Golden, do you think I would ask you if anybody else was in town?"

SALT LAKE WASN'T BUILT IN A DAY

President Heber J. Grant hosted some wealthy financiers from the East Coast. He needed someone to show them around the city while he met with Church accountants. J. Golden reluctantly agreed to show them the sights.

They boarded a bus. First they went by the

McCune Mansion on Second North. One of the
financiers asked, "How many years did it take
them to build this mansion?" Golden responded,
"It took them four years to build this place." The
financier said, "We could have done it in two
years back East."

It was obvious to Golden that these men from
the East did not understand the difficult trials
and circumstances of early pioneer times.

Next Golden took them to the grand City and
County Building. The same financier asked how

long it took to construct this building. Golden
stated, "Seven years." The financier quipped,
"We could have built it in five years back East."
This was beginning to bother Golden.

They turned up Main Street in the direction of
the Temple and the Hotel Utah. As the group
was passing Temple Square, Golden didn't say
anything. The outspoken financier pointed to the
Temple and said, "Hey, what's that building
over there?"

Golden looked at the building in complete and
utter astonishment. "Damned if I know. It
wasn't there yesterday!"

SACRIFICIAL GOAT

Golden on occasion signed his letters to
members of the Church, "Faithfully your
brother, J. Golden Kimball, Scapegoat of the
Church."

SUITS ME

One day Golden went into ZCMI to buy a suit. It is important to remember how very tall (6'4") and thin (145 lbs) he was. He walked into the men's clothing department and rifled through the racks, looking at suits.

A salesman came up and said, "May I help you, sir?"

Golden said, "Yes, I would like to see a suit that would fit me."

The salesman made a quick appraisal of Golden's scrawny frame and responded, "Hell, so would I."

They both laughed.

MAYBE A 36 XXXXL

THE ONE THAT
GOT AWAY

President Spencer W. Kimball said that prior to his being a stake president in Thatcher, Arizona, a small, 70-year-old Jewish-German investigator finally decided to join the Church. He insisted that J. Golden Kimball baptize him.

Golden remembered who this man was and said he would gladly do it.

Golden went down to Arizona. President Kimball said they drove out to a grove of poplar trees where there was a stream. It was during spring runoff and there was a strong current in the stream. President Kimball said it was a beautiful spot and the trees were just leafing out. He added that all the members from Thatcher gathered around the bank to watch Golden take this man into the waters of baptism.

Golden said the baptismal prayer and immersed the brother into the water. The strong current snatched the new convert away and Golden raised his empty hands. "Damn, I lost him!"

The faithful members from Thatcher jumped

into the water, women and men, fully clothed. They searched until they found him, spurting water like a small whale about 10 yards downstream.

President Kimball said he would never forget that particular baptism.

PLAY BALL!

This story happened at one of the stake conferences J. Golden presided over in St. George during the summer of 1926.

There was no air conditioning of any kind in those days. The Sunday morning session went just fine, no problem. Then the 2:00 session came and there were not as many people there as had been to the morning session. J.  Golden asked the local authorities, "Where are all the people? Is it just too hot?"

They said, "No, there's a very important baseball game going on out at the ballpark."

Brother Kimball got up and said, "We're going to dismiss from here and we'll meet out at the ballpark." It was about a four-block walk. J. Golden led the procession. The small congregation filed into the bleachers while J.

Golden walked up to the umpire.

"I'm taking over this game!" he said.

J. Golden stood at home plate and gave his sermon. When he got to the end, he said, "In the name of Jesus Christ, Amen. Play ball!"

He then went up into the stands and watched the rest of the game with the congregation.

SEVEN SAD
SALINA SISTERS

There was a family of seven young sisters in Salina. They were extremely close. The youngest caught pneumonia and died. The whole family was stricken by this tragic loss. The sisters were inconsolable.

In planning the funeral, the parents wrote Uncle Golden and asked him, as an old family friend, to be the principal speaker. Golden accepted.

He drove to Salina on the appointed day. When he walked into the crowded chapel, he was greeted by the parents but none of the daughters. Golden asked where they were, and the father said they were still at home, unable to pull themselves together. Golden told them not to begin the meeting until he returned.

He walked to the family's home. He found the daughters in the living room in a mournful and weeping state. He offered his condolences to each of them and as he left, he paused at the door and said, "May I give you sisters some advice? I would suggest you wash your faces, put on a little makeup, comb your hair and get into your best dresses. Otherwise, the congregation down at the chapel will think the pretty one died."

LEADETH ME INTO TEMPTATION...

A successful businessman called as stake president in California spoke before Golden in a stake conference. The new stake president chose as his subject how the Lord had tempted him with great wealth all of his life, but he had resisted.

"Brothers and Sisters, I could have tripled my wealth on several occasions. The Lord tempted me with great wealth, but I resisted because I knew what it would do to me. I was tempted to invest in unproven oil fields, gold mines and stock investments. All could have given me wealth untold, but I resisted the temptation!"

He went along on this theme of being tempted for the better part of an hour before he finally bore his testimony and sat down.

Golden was up next. He looked at the audience with a wry smile and said, "I wish to hell the Lord would tempt me just once!"

SILENCE IS GOLDEN

Uncle Golden spoke at a ward conference. One man in the audience had little patience with anyone, especially a General Authority, telling him how to live his life.

When Golden finished his talk, sure enough the man went up to him while he was still on the stand and told him he did not appreciate being told what to do by any Church leader. He said he was fully capable of reading the scriptures and deciding for himself how to live his own life, thank you.

Golden listened without interrupting. He finally asked the man to come down and see him at his office the next day.

The man showed up at the appointed time all set for a good confrontation. Golden's secretary invited him into the office and told him to sit down. Golden was on the phone at the time and continued to talk. He then did some paperwork without saying a word to the man.

Finally, Golden got up and walked to the window and looked down on South Temple Street for some time. He then asked the man to join him at the window

As they stood there, Golden said, "You see those men down there sweeping up horse turds? I'd be doing the same damn thing if I hadn't learned to keep my mouth shut some of the time. Do you understand what the hell I'm trying to tell you?"

The brother got the message.

FLEECE MY SHEEP

The shady ethics of some LDS businessmen concerned Uncle Golden. He often talked of their deceptive speech and sly behavior in business dealings.

"Such brethren will work you over and then leave you penniless, my friends. They are like anyone else. The only difference is they will do it to you to organ music."

WHISTLE STOPS

An elderly gentleman from Holladay recalled the first time he heard Uncle Golden speak. "Brother Joseph Fielding Smith was the first speaker of the conference and he really let us have it. He berated us for over an hour. He left us with the clear impression that none of us would make it in the next life.

"When Golden got up, he won the audience over by simply saying, 'Brother Smith has just told you how you're all on a train headed straight to Hell. Let me make a few suggestions how you might jump off at the next station.'"

THE GOSPEL TRUTH

J. Golden said to a good friend in his later years, "Well, Charlie, it won't be long now until we'll go find out if all this stuff we've been preaching all these years is true."

AFTERWARD

J. Golden Kimball died tragically on September 2, 1938, the only General Authority ever to die in a car accident. Thirty thousand people turned out for his funeral. Gentiles and Mormons were united in lamenting the passing of this truly great and beloved man. Even the Salt Lake Tribune, notorious at that time for heaping abuse on Mormon leaders, printed the following:

The Church, of which he was an honored member and a high official, may never have another like him. He was frank, outspoken, and fearless in his utterances. His discourses scintillated with original observations which occasionally disturbed some of his hearers, but never failed to convey his honest thoughts. Rich and

risible are the stories told of his apt retorts
and pointed remarks. His genial,
wholesome nature will be remembered
long and his quaint sayings repeated after
many solemn visages and doleful homilies
are forgotten.

There was but one J. Golden Kimball. He
was respected, beloved, and enjoyed by all
with whom he made contact. His passing
is a distinct loss to his circle, his Church,
his community and his commonwealth.

PUBLISHER'S NOTE

If you have any J. Golden Kimball stories that you wish to share with James Kimball and Whitehorse Books, please email them to:

Whitehorse Books c/o mnreiser@aol.com

or send them by regular mail to:

James Kimball
36 Dartmoor Place
Salt Lake City, Utah 84103